D1799087

$6.50

Faces of Fiji

FRONTISPIECE *(overleaf)*

LIMA BULAMAIBAU was born at Lautoka twenty-six years ago. Her mother is part Fijian, Tongan, Lauan and German-Jewish. Her father is a full-blooded Fijian.

FACES
OF
FIJI

Kristin Zambucka

A. H. & A. W. Reed
Wellington / Sydney / London

First published 1974

A.H. & A.W. REED LTD
182 Wakefield Street, Wellington
51 Whiting Street, Artarmon, NSW 2064
11 Southampton Row, London WC1B 5HA
also
29 Dacre Street, Auckland
165 Cashel Street, Christchurch

© 1974 Kristin Zambucka

All rights reserved. No part of this publication
may be reproduced, stored in a retrieval system
or transmitted in any form or by any means
electronic, mechanical, photocopying, recording
or otherwise without the prior written permission
of the publishers.

ISBN 0 589 00869 2

Printed and bound by
Kyodo Printing Company Ltd, Tokyo

ACKNOWLEDGMENTS

My thanks to Mr Bill Clark and his staff at the Korolevu Beach Hotel for
all their help and for giving me a "home away from home". Thanks to
Mr and Mrs Otto at Rakiraki for their help and hospitality. My gratitude
to the entire staff, past and present, of the Fiji Visitors' Bureau for help
too extensive to mention, during my many visits to Suva. And my thanks
to all the people in Fiji who put themselves out to help me compile this
book—especially the subjects themselves.

INTRODUCTION

FIJI is a feast of colour—a mixture of races, cultures and vivid pictures that stay with you long after you leave the island.

I compiled this collection of portraits and stories over two years of intermittent visits to the island of Viti Levu, where most of the population of Fiji is concentrated. Never was there a shortage of colourful subjects.

During my numerous journeys around the island, when the odd puncture brought me to a rumbling halt, so many drivers gallantly stopped to help me in every possible way. Their concern was genuine, and the kindness of the island people of all racial backgrounds touched me on many occasions. Small things, indicative of a human warmth that is so sadly lacking now from the societies of more "advanced" countries of the world.

In late 1972 Hurricane Bebe cruelly struck Fiji. Raging winds flattened *bures* (Fijian houses), blew stout mango trees over, and caused landslides. Taro crops were ruined, and villagers in the mountainous interior of Viti Levu were cut off from civilisation for several days, stranded by seas of mud. The sea came up and claimed the dance floor at the Korolevu Beach Hotel, my base for so long.

Wanting to join European friends in Nadi just before the big blow reached its height, I was warned about flying trees. I commissioned a taxi as far as Korolevu as flights from Nausori had all been cancelled, and my own delicate Fiat was safely stored between concrete walls in Suva.

"Don't go on." I was warned again when I reached Korolevu, but a daring young Muslim driver took me on to Nadi. Snapped-off palm fronds were blowing everywhere along the road; Fijian villagers and Indian families were battening windows, storing belongings, and taking what ever precautions they could before they were at the mercy of Bebe's breath.

That night, while the hurricane was at its full, howling force, my friends and I helped an Indian family mop us seeping water as the louvre windows of their concrete building blew in one by one. Iron roofs screeched as they were ripped off houses up the road, and flung around like paper.

The next morning brought an eerie stillness, and people carefully ventured out of doors (that's if they could open them against the banked-up mud and rubbish blown against them).

Trees were uprooted along the road to the airport, whole canefields had been lifted up and thrown on the roadway, and metal telegraph poles were twisted as if by a giant hand, their electric wires swinging dangerously low.

An assortment of debris, some with people clinging to it, floated bravely down the swollen Nadi River. The brown water that had spilt over its banks and right through the town went down quickly, and by midday we went walking, or sliding, through the eight inches of mud that had settled on the main street of Nadi town and oozed its way into shops, staining and ruining goods.

The buoyancy of spirits of the Indian and Fijian people at this time was incredible. Many of them had lost everything.

That was a time of trouble in Fiji, of adversity. There were other seasons, other feelings and scenes of a different hue.

I sat in a darkened hut one night with a firewalking Indian priest near the temple where he would walk on fire the next day. He was preparing himself to feel no pain. It was pitch-black all around; only an oil lamp flickered on the fine contours of his ascetic face.

The rituals began next day in honour of the goddess Durga (in Hindu mythology she created man by rubbing her right arm, and woman by rubbing her left arm). The atmosphere in the temple at Wailekutu was charged with an unearthly presence as piano wire was pushed through the skin of Indian devotees, their shoulders and necks were pierced, and they felt nothing. Their tongues were pierced with metal skewers. Some were walking with vases of flowers suspended from spikes in their tongues, their eyes grazed. Their goddess was close by and she protected them

Continued page 8

PLATE 1: KELENI is an orphan, but she leads a carefree life.

In her village in Nadroga district, Viti Levu, she plays under nodding palm trees, and wades in a calm lagoon, often up to her neck in cool water, gathering the lilac flowers of water lilies that cluster thickly in their lush green leaves on the water's dark surface.

Sometimes Keleni and her "gang" from the village prefer to splash boisteriously in the nearby sea, while the men pull in their heavy nets; a squirming, wriggling mass of captured silver bodies. Later in the day there will be fresh fish—*walu, saga, ogo* (barracuda) and mullet, to eat with boiled *dalo* and yams.

The mangoes are in season, so the children can feast—long red 'carrot" mangoes are the sweetest, and the huge trees have dropped their exotic fruit everywhere, just to be picked up.

Agile village boys easily climb the palm trees, clinging to the ridged, grey trunks with their strong brown feet, until they reach the web of leafy fronds at the top, with the bunches of husky fruit hanging below them. Green coconuts are knocked down and broken open with a rock, or carefully hacked with a cane knife, so that their sweet milk can be sucked into dry young throats after playtime.

The warm starry night finds Keleni sleeping beside her adopted family in a thatched *bure*, their bodies stretched out on silky, handwoven mats.

Under the rules of communal life in a Fijian village, orphaned children are taken care of beside the sick and the aged.

Keleni is seven now. Soon she will learn the crafts of her village—how to weave baskets from coconut leaves, how to make fine mats from rolls of *voivoi* plant, and there may be instruction in the age-old craft of making *tapa* cloth, or *masi*, as the Fijians call their own indigenous art form. The elders of the village have noticed that Keleni shows an aptitude for art. She will be taught to soak the white inner bark of the paper mulberry tree, and beat it with a wooden mallet to paper thinness, and to cut a stencil from strips of banana leaves, and mix her own colours from natural pigments. She will be taught to dream up her own designs and paint them on the cloth.

Designs are traditional and intricate. They vary from island to island and are often unique to each *masi* maker. The panels may be displayed on the wall, the bed or the floor, and traditionally pieces of *masi* may be worn at a wedding or funeral.

from harm. Sleekhaired women in marigold saris picked *gulagula* (a sort of small doughnut) from a pan of boiling ghee with their bare fingers— they were not scalded. A university professor measured the heat of the boiling ghee at 130°C.

A group of young men and women danced barefoot on the razor-sharp blades of fifteen upturned cane knives fixed to a wooden platform. Their vulnerable feet were not cut. They walked calmly away, their hands joined in prayer.

The firewalkers approached, some of them women, holding young children in their arms. The crashing and beating of the goatskin drums was deafening, but hypnotic, as they walked through the oblong pit of hot ashes. Their gaits differed, some arched their bodies and rushed through; some walked slowly, erect, with fixed eyes; some turned again and again in the steps of a private dance.

There is a touching faith among poor Indian families who journey from afar just to watch the rituals and gaze on their beloved goddess, heavily garlanded with red and gold flowers. Her garishly painted face achieves a benign expression as she promises fertility and good fortune to those who love her. Offerings of precious food are tenderly placed in brass bowls at her feet, while incense wafts its thin smoke around her plaster head.

The Fijian firewalk is such a different scene. Shouting for joy, holding hands and singing, the islanders of Beqa perform in more primitive surroundings. Their temple is the leafy foliage all around, so close to the life force of their fertile island with its lush greenery. The Beqans have faith in their river god who gave them the gift of immunity from fire after his life was spared by a hunter. He had appeared as an eel in a river that day.

Continued page 10

PLATE 2: TEVITA D. QIO is sixty-three years old and the *ratu* (chief) of four villages in the Nadroga district of Viti Levu.

His wife is the daughter of a chief in the village of Namosi, fifty miles away. The couple have five children—four sons and a daughter. The eldest son will become the *ratu* when Tevita dies.

The *ratu* spoke of his people, the Fijians who worhsip many gods still co-existing with the prevalent Christianity on the island. One belief has nothing to do with the other, they say.

"We believe in our old songs, legends and poems," Tevita said. *"Our people had no written language, so all our history was passed by word of mouth. I think there were two separate groups of Fijians who came to these shores, long ago. This is suggested by the dialects of our language. If I speak my dialect over on the eastern side, I'm not understood.*

"This island, Viti Levu, could have been the first home of the Fijians, and Vuda (near Nadi) is the source. That's where they landed, the chiefs, and their families, and they followed the ridge of the Tualeita mountain range until they reached Nakauvadra on the Ra side, their first home. Viti Levu means to break; the big job of breaking the branches to make their way.

"All our ancestors came from Africa—from different areas of that continent, but all from Africa. Many of our most ancient songs and mekes tell of Tanganyika."

Carefully the islanders place their feet on whitehot rocks. The rush of intense heat pushes spectators back as they creep to within ten feet, nervously positioning their cameras for a once-in-a-lifetime shot of man defying the elements.

So many memories crowd back . . .

Muslims in their proud white mosques, facing Mecca, and raising their voices in salute to Allah . . .

Sikhs with their uncut hair bound up in brightly coloured turbans, offering hospitality to all who come by their temples, regardless of race or creed . . .

Indian widows in flimsy white saris, walking by the roadside like ghosts, or stirring a bubbling goat-meat curry in a pan on a primitive primus stove in a shanty dwelling near Nausori . . .

The Fijian villages where hibiscus bushes bloom in gaudy abundance and pigs, chickens, and countless stray dogs wander about . . .

The silky, cool feeling of woven mats beneath your feet as you enter a shaded *bure*, and an elder offers you *yangona* (*kava*) in a coconut bowl; the lavishness of food at a Chinese wedding in Tamavua Heights; the dignity of Tongans in the Suva streets; the excitement and peculiar mixture of smells in the early morning at the markets—copra, fresh vegetables with brown earth clinging to them, wet fish, and dry straw matting; the air of anticipation at Suva Wharf as a huge passenger liner edges her way in, and most of the town turns out in welcome while the Fiji Police Band plays lustily in their distinctive white *sulus*.

Indian movies with incomprehensive plots and deafening soundtracks, in air conditioned theatres, where exotic smells of garlic and brilliantined hair battle their way through the darkened atmosphere . . .

Oily turtle meat cooked in banana leaves; *kokoda* (raw fish in coconut

Continued page 12

PLATE 3:   ADI (meaning lady) MERESENI KURUVADRA is aged between 102 and 105, and lives in the village of NAVOCI, half a mile from Nadi. She was born in the Nausori highlands, the daughter of a chief, Ratu Simeli Koli.

She has been blind for seven years.

Mereseni married and had eight children—five sons and three daughters. One of her sons is Ratu Inoke Davu, and in the coolness of the old lady's *bure* at Navoci we discussed the matrilineal descent of the Melanesian people. There are no hereditary high chiefs to the true Melanesian; the system of high chiefs is of Polynesian origin, and therefore patrilineal. The Fijians have long used a combination of both systems, and elaborate ceremonies are held when a new chief is inaugurated.

A Fijian's rank depends upon his birth and both his parents' family descent. These can be differences of rank between two high-born chiefs fathered by the same man, if the mother of one is from a better family than the other. A chief can be elevated to a higher rank than his own father if his mother is sufficiently *marama* (high-born).

10

milk); *rou-rou* (the mushy, cooked green leaves of the *dalo*); fresh pine-apple; sticks of sugar cane snapped off along the road to Lautoka and offered by eager, young, brown hands ...

The Somerset Maugham atmosphere of the old Oceanic Hotel, and the Grand Pacific with its wooden slatted doors, whirling fans cooling overhead, and pale pink exterior placed carefully among green palms; nearby the gently lapping sounds of Suva Bay.

These are some memories of my visits to Fiji. When the mind starts churning them out they are never ending; all the pictures are indelible.

Kristin Zambucka
Viseisei Village, Fiji, 1973

THE FIJIANS

THE TRADITIONAL COMMUNITY LIFE of the Fijian village has advantages which still exist today. Orphans are readily taken care of; the sick, aged and infirm are never considered a burden; and food is always equally shared.

The Fijian can still easily live off the land around his village. Root crops thrive and there are coconuts, pineapple, mangoes in season, bananas and other fruits. What Fiji lacks in animal meats is amply compensated for by the abundance of fish in the sea.

More and more, the Fijians in recent times have broken away from the ties of village life to work individually in the towns, or to start their own small farms. So the powers and authorities of the village chiefs are gradually lessening.

PLATE 4: THIS FIJIAN WOMAN brings vegetables from her village daily to sell at the Suva market—*dalo*, yams, tapioca, Chinese cabbage and lettuce.

Often she dives in the Rewa River to collect *kai*, fresh-water shellfish, which sell readily.

She sits on a large mat on the outside of the market building, with her piles of fresh produce beside her, bartering and chatting with the customers who amble by.

Her "cigar" is made of rolled and dried banana leaves.

BEQA ISLAND, lying off the southernmost point of Viti Levu, is the home of the firewalkers. These Fijians walk on white-hot rocks, laughing and shouting as though they enjoy a walk which would roast the soles off foreign feet.

Their own name for their island is Vilavilairevo, which means "jumping into the ovens".

About 300 years ago, according to the old *bete* (priest), a hunter on Beqa spared the life of an eel. In reality the eel was a river god who had changed form.

To show his gratitude, the god bestowed the gift of immunity from fire upon all the people of Beqa. If they prepare themselves correctly, they can walk on fire without being burnt.

They must be celibate for at least a week before the firewalk, and neither the white flesh nor the milk of the coconut must be touched during that time.

They sat close together in a leafy shack made of palm fronds, and waited. This group of Beqans was all male, although their women sometimes walk on fire with them.

One of these firewalkers was only nine years old. Others were aged twelve, thirteen and fifteen. The rest were mature men. Most of them were quietly reading; a few turned the pages of a Bible, others were reading comic books and laughing at Charlie Brown.

But whatever the spirit that pervaded that place, it had settled as a quiet confidence over all of them. There was a strong faith in something and it hung around them like a protective aura. Outside, the pit was glowing. The heat rose and flung back anyone who approached to within a few yards. The white-hot bed of rocks shimmered, waiting for the Beqans to defy its heat.

Eventually they jogged in single file from their shack, whooping what sounded like cries of pure joy. Holding hands they placed their feet on the hot rocks, until they were all inside the pit. They balanced on the fiery stones, waving their arms about and singing. Bundles of greenery were thrown in around their feet, and thick blue clouds of steam rose to engulf their skirted figures. Their faith had triumphed again.

The Beqans sat on the grass after the firewalk and held up the soles of their feet for all to see. There were traces of grey ash on the skin, but it was cool to the touch, although a couple of minutes before it had apparently been cooked. There was no sign of any burns. Even the tinder-dry anklets of the sacred plant, *voivoi*, did not ignite, as they performed their fiery dance.

The river god had kept his ancient promise of protection.

PLATE 5: FIREWALKER *"I placed my foot on the white-hot rock, not heel first then toe, but flat. I placed the whole of my foot down, and the glowing rock felt cool, even slippery, so I walked on. I felt no feeling of heat at all."*

THE INDIANS

FROM 1879 when the first Indians arrived in Fiji—481 of them as indentured labourers—their numbers have increased until today there are more than 272,000 Indians living in Fiji. They outnumber all other racial groups by far, even the Fijians.

They are keen business people and many operate thriving commercial enterprises throughout the Fiji islands. Others have farms, grow rice or vegetables, or raise stock. Through the hard work of their fathers, many have acquired higher education and become doctors, lawyers and teachers.

Most of these Indians are descended from the 40,000 workers who decided to remain in Fiji after their labour contracts expired *circa* 1920.

All the religions they had known in the old country were brought to Fiji in the minds and hearts of those early toilers. There are Sikh, Muslim and Hindu temples throughout Fiji. A few Indians are Christians.

PLATE 6: THERE ARE FOUR FEATURES by which a Sikh may be recognised:
1. On his wrist he wears a silver bangle;
2. He grows a beard;
3. His long hair is never cut;
4. He winds a brightly-coloured turban around his head to bind up his hair.

Occasionally (although not often these days) a sword or dagger may be seen hanging from his belt.

Sikhs are known as friendly, generous people who offer hospitality to all. A room at the back of the temple at Lautoka has ten wooden beds waiting for visitors who wish to stay overnight, regardless of religion or creed.

Their Garthan or Bible also dictates that they never cut their hair throughout their lives.

PLATE 7: SHAKUNTALA's grandparents were brought to Fiji from northern India in the 1880s, as indentured labourers for the sugar industry.

Shakuntala's wedding was an arranged marriage to a Hindu boy of suitable family background. The ceremony began with the offering of tea to the hundreds of guests, resplendent in their best clothes; the multi-coloured saris of the women gaudy and exotic against the green lawns of the temple grounds.

Then the wedding presents, a variety of goods ranging from furniture to crockery, clothes and money, were presented to the young couple.

Indian music was played on a loudspeaker while the gifts were admired. Suddenly this music stopped to be replaced by the plaintive notes of a *bansuri* (flute) and drum accompaniment.

The centuries-old Hindu wedding ceremony had begun inside the *mundup* (temple)

The bride was shy. Her dark face was hidden behind the folds of a golden veil to match the gold sari draped carefully around her slim body.

Both bride and groom wore garlands of white flowers around their necks. The young man was handsome. He rubbed his hand nervously against the smooth yellow satin of his long wedding shirt pulled in around his waist by a red sash.

When they were finally declared man and wife, the bride's sari was tied to the end of her new husband's sash, (they were united now) and the couple walked slowly around the temple seven times.

18

PLATE 8: RAM DUT is a Sadhu, a Hindu holy man. He came to work in the canefields of Fiji during the indentured labour period.

He was born at Kisunpur in northern India one hundred years ago, and left home at the age of fourteen, never to return.

His mind wandered back to those early days of relentless work under the blazing sun.

"We worked every day," he said. *"Cutting cane from first light to sunset, for the wages of 6d a day."*

Ram Dut has lived at Nausori, a market town twelve miles from Suva, ever since those days.

All his contemporaries are dead. He has outlived all his friends from the canefield days—days that left welts across the backs of many of the Indian labourers. The agents that lured them to the "new land of plenty" were determined to get the most out of them, and the whip was very persuasive to the tender bodies of young Indian boys. Some of them were from Brahmin families and had never known work in their lives. They soon learned.

The strain was too much for some. Homesickness combined with work and conditions that were unbearable caused many a spirit to break. Suicide was widespread. Only the very strong survived.

Some passers-by, recognising the holy man, asked him where his temple was, so that they might visit.

"My temple is all around me," the old man replied in English. And the world bustled past him as he sat cross-legged on the sidewalk of Nausori's main street.

PLATE 9: RAMPARAI DAYARAM is "about 100". She was born in northern India and came to Fiji with her parents when she was a small child. Widowed many years ago, she raised two children, working the long hours typical of Indian housewives.

I noticed that the back of the old lady's left hand was curiously tattooed with an intricate lacy pattern that extended halfway down her fingers. It was put there when Ramparai was in her teens, and has no particular significance that she knows of— just decoration.

OTHER ISLANDERS

THERE ARE more than 8,000 "other islanders" living in Fiji today. Even before Indian labour was brought in, thousands of people from the New Hebrides, the Solomons and the Gilbert and Ellice groups were lured to Fiji to work on sugar and cotton plantations. Then in the early 1900s, with no immigration restrictions to inhibit them, many more poured in from Tonga, Samoa, and other parts of the Pacific.

PLATE 10: MARIE TIVAO was born at Malhaha, and is a pure-blooded Rotuman.

EARLY EXPLORATION

MANY EXPLORERS did nothing but observe and chart the Fijian islands from afar. The few who did venture ashore carried away terrifying tales of cannibalism and savagery.

In 1643 ABEL TASMAN saw the northern tip of Tavenui from his small ship, and sailed away due north of the Lau group. He reported that the hazardous coral reefs in the area should be avoided by sailing ships.

CAPTAIN COOK, on his second voyage of discovery in the Pacific sighted Vatoa, a small island in southern Lau, on 2 June 1774. He warned future seafarers of a treacherous reef nearby.

After the mutiny on the *Bounty*, CAPTAIN BLIGH was ungallantly put off his own ship by the mutineers, and forced to navigate the *Bounty*'s long-boat for more than 3,000 miles through the Fiji islands until he reached Java. Bligh was an officer on Cook's third and last voyage, and having heard all the horror stories of cannibalism as practised by the Fijians, he made no attempt to land. At least two canoes of Fijian warriors chased him as he headed for the open sea with Viti Levu in full view on his port-side. Safely back in London, Captain Bligh published a chart of the Fiji islands, and for some time the group was known as Bligh's Islands.

The FIRST EUROPEANS to venture ashore and live among the Fijians were either shipwrecked sailors or runaway convicts from Australia. The chiefs of the villages that sheltered them acquired their first knowledge of the white man's guns from these men. In 1805 the sandalwood trade began and this business flourished for the seafarers for ten years until all the sandalwood trees were depleted. The visitors then turned their attention to bêche de mer, with the hope of making their fortunes. The Christian missionaries began to arrive and by the 1830s some permanent traders had opened stores at Levuka, the old capital on the island of Ovalau.

PLATE 11: THIS OLD TONGAN LADY claims descent from the fighting chiefs of Tonga who came to Fiji in 1853 and supported the Tongan Prince Ma'afu who challenged the supremacy of Cakobau, the paramount chief in Fiji.

As early as 1840 there were numerous communities of Tongans living in the Fiji islands. At that period a third of the population of the island of Lakeba was Tongan.

Often the Tongan interference in Fijian affairs was considered a menace by the Fijian high chiefs of the day, although some of the Tongan chiefs were feared and influential, and their advice was often sought during that period of unrest in Fiji.

Their canoes were in demand too for the Tongan seamen were very skilled and daring, venturing much farther afield than the Fijians, who seldom sailed out of sight of their homeland.

Tongans are Polynesian. They have long, wavy hair and light golden skins. (By comparison the Fijian of Melanesian origin has frizzy hair and a darker skin.) The Polynesians tend to carry more fat on their bodies than the Fijians who are generally tall, lean and big-boned.

THE CHINESE

THE CHINESE PEOPLE entered Fiji as free settlers. There was no restriction on immigration in 1911, when they began to journey from China to settle as merchants, market gardeners and shopkeepers. There are about 5,500 Chinese citizens in Fiji today.

PLATE 12: MAY LAAN YEE was born in Nasea, Labasa in 1953.

Her parents brought her to Suva when she was a baby, and she remembers nothing of her home town. Both her parents are from Canton, in China.

In 1928 her grandfather and father arrived in Fiji together; her father at the time was sixteen.

Nine years later he returned to Canton to marry, but returned to Fiji alone. His wife didn't join him for fifteen years. The year after she arrived, May Laan was born.

The Yee family have worked for many years as storekeepers, and they once owned and operated a farm at Tamavua.

THE EUROPEANS

FROM THE LATE 1890s onwards, the plantation industry boomed. The Europeans established themselves on large areas of land where they grew coconuts, bananas and sugar.

After the indentured Indian labourers became free settlers in 1920, the big sugar plantations were divided into smaller holdings, and the number of individual banana growers began to dwindle. Today only a few European coconut planters remain.

However, the European population in Fiji continues to grow, numbering today almost 5,000.

PLATE 13: BEATRICE FRANCES HENRIETTA CHARLOTTE PARHAM was four years old when the Parham family came to Fiji from New Zealand to run a coconut plantation. It was just after World War I, and Beatrice recalls those early days:

"Life for the girls in our family was far from what it had been in New Zealand. The coconut plantation was very isolated, and grass houses were not the best types of residences during a hurricane season. However there was always something of interest to study and draw, or make notes about. In addition there was the daily bread-making and other household chores. Money was scarce, but there was much in the ties of family life which no money could buy. Then came the shadow of a much loved father's illness and death. For me it marked the end of hope for medical studies overseas. However, with the leadership of a wonderful mother came other opportunities for serving God and those in need."

World War II brought the Civil Defence Service to Suva (not then a city) with the duties of Assistant Warden for Beatrice. She was under the command of the Town Clerk and took care of the women and children while overseeing one of the town's air raid shelters.

OTHER REED BOOKS

ART AND LIFE IN POLYNESIA *by T. Barrow*
Polynesian art is viewed directly in relation to life by presenting, with caption and comment, an extensive range of colour and black and white illustrations. The work is the result of Dr Barrow's twenty years as a museum ethnologist; a lifelong fascination with the Pacific peoples, and extensive scientific research.

SOUTH PACIFIC *by Jack and Dorothy Fields*
From the thousands of colour slides he has taken over a twenty-year period, photographer Jack Fields has chosen a selection to capture the immense diversity and the magic and splendour of the islands and islanders, while his wife Dorothy has written a complementary and evocative text. Together they have created a record that is truly unique in the literature of Oceania.

FIJI IN COLOUR *by James Siers*
This is the new enlarged and revised edition, containing more splendid colour pictures than ever, of James Siers's *Fiji in Colour* first published in 1969. Many beautiful colour plates.

POLYNESIA IN COLOUR *by James Siers*
A colourful survey of the most romantic island groups scattered over the South Pacific. The colour photographs are superb and the text gives a fascinating insight into early European exploration and provides up-to-date information on tourist facilities throughout the area.

SAMOA IN COLOUR *by James Siers*
This lively and informative book on both Eastern and Western Samoa is full of magnificent colour photographs. The beauty of the islands and the warmth and vivacity of their people are strikingly evoked, along with a comprehensive introduction to their history.

TAHITI IN COLOUR *by James Siers*
Following a lively introduction to the history of the Tahitians and a discussion of Polynesian migration, the author takes the reader on a journey to all the main islands of the Society group.

NEW ZEALAND *by Walter Imber and Prof. K. Cumberland*
The most lavish and impressive of all colour books published about New Zealand. It combines the dramatic view of New Zealand by a continental photographer with an informative text written by a team of scholars. The beauty of New Zealand is excitingly portrayed in the photographs, and the text presents an extensive and factual impression of land and people.